# From

## Lute to Uke
### Early Music for Ukulele
ARRANGED AND PERFORMED BY TONY MIZEN

To access audio visit:
**www.halleonard.com/mylibrary**
Enter Code
3043-1632-0059-3277

HAL•LEONARD® CORPORATION

7777 W. BLUEMOUND RD. P.O. BOX 13819 MILWAUKEE, WI 53213

Edited by Ronny S. Schiff
Cover and Art Direction by Elizabeth Maihock Beloff
Graphics and Music Typography by John Russell Duffy and Charylu Roberts
Cover Ukulele Photo by Rick Scanlan

# Foreword

**M**ost of the initial ideas for the ukulele songbooks we've published over the years have originated from within, meaning from Liz and me. This time the idea of arranging early lute music for ukulele came from Tony Mizen, the arranger and author of this songbook, via his email from England, which concluded with, "I hope you will consider this a worthwhile project." After listening to some of Tony's sample arrangements, it seemed worthwhile indeed.

As you will hear on the audio tracks, the ukulele is surprisingly good at expressing the beauty of these four- and five-hundred year-old pieces. Tony, working primarily from guitar reductions, shrinks the arrangements even further to accommodate reentrant (high G) GCEA tuning. In so doing, he clearly makes the case for early music on the uke.

As with the *John King: Classical Ukulele* songbook we published in 2004, the pieces are presented both as notated music and in ukulele tablature, which makes it especially easy to read for non-musicians. While most intermediate players should find much to enjoy here, there are many pieces arranged with the advanced beginner in mind.

A big thank you to Tony Mizen for suggesting this songbook and proving that in this interconnected world, inspiration can come from anywhere. Also, thanks to Paul Baker, Diabolus in Musica, and, as always to our team of regulars, Ronny, Charylu and Liz...for all that you do.

Enjoy!

—Jim Beloff
September 2011

**Also available: (Songbooks)** *Jumpin' Jim's Ukulele Favorites; Jumpin' Jim's Ukulele Tips 'n' Tunes; Jumpin' Jim's Ukulele Gems; Jumpin' Jim's Ukulele Christmas; Jumpin' Jim's '60s Uke-In; Jumpin' Jim's Gone Hawaiian; Jumpin' Jim's Camp Ukulele; Jumpin' Jim's Ukulele Masters: Lyle Ritz; Jumpin' Jim's Ukulele Beach Party; Jumpin' Jim's Ukulele Masters: Herb Ohta; Jumpin' Jim's Ukulele Masters: Lyle Ritz Solos; Jumpin' Jim's Ukulele Spirit; Jumpin' Jim's Gone Hollywood; Jumpin' Jim's Ukulele Island; Jumpin' Jim's Ukulele Masters: John King—The Classical Ukulele; Jumpin' Jim's Ukulele Country; Jumpin' Jim's The Bari Best; Ukulele Fretboard Roadmaps* (with Fred Sokolow); *Jumpin' Jim's Happy Holidays; Jumpin' Jim's Ukulele Masters: Lyle Lite; Blues Ukulele; Bluegrass Ukulele; The Daily Ukulele.* **(Pictorial History)** *The Ukulele: A Visual History.*

Visit us on the web at ***www.fleamarketmusic.com***

# Biography

Tony Mizen began playing the guitar at the age of fourteen. After several years of strumming chords, he found himself drawn to flamenco and then classical guitar, with inspiration from several excellent teachers. He won first place four years in a row at a guitar festival in Kent and, after passing his performer's diploma, he started teaching the guitar full time in various schools.

Several years ago, Tony was asked if he could teach the ukulele. He knew nothing about the instrument but agreed to the task, swiftly buying a ukulele and instruction book. Since that day, the ukulele has been an absorbing interest for Tony. He was delighted to discover the Victoria College of Music in London, UK, which takes the instrument seriously enough to produce an entire exam syllabus. Tony took the Performer's Diploma in 2010, passing with Distinction. He is the first person in the UK to have a diploma in the ukulele.

# Credits

I am grateful for everyone who was involved in this project. I had a great time doing it.

The audio that is included in this book was recorded at Audio Sorcery studios near Tunbridge Wells, Kent, United Kingdom. It was recorded and mastered by Dale Nash during April 2011. The music was engraved by John Duffy in Edinburgh, UK, with polishing by Charylu Roberts in the USA. The photograph was by St.John Asprey and I had some great help with my research on the pieces from Piers Wilson, who also suggested that I send the material to Jim Beloff. Many thanks to everyone involved, especially Jim! Finally, a big thank you to my wife, Lisa Mizen for all her support.

# The History Of The Lute

In analyzing the history of musical instruments, it is helpful to study them in the same way that an evolutionary biologist studies animals, both living and extinct. If you look at a camel and a llama for example, you can see certain similarities but also many differences. Their differences are the result of migration and adaptation to different environments until a slow accumulation of change creates two distinct species.

In applying this model to the evolution of the lute, we can see that the Arabian oud looks like a lute in many ways and it is logical to suppose a connection between the two. The Arabian instrument has no frets and is plucked with a quill that produces a sound so beautifully dark, so primal that it is difficult to describe. This instrument and its music found its way to Spain during the time of the Moorish occupation. It "bred" with the native Spanish music and evolved eventually into a unique music and dance species called *Flamenco*.

The oud then migrated to other European countries, adapting to new regions and cultures. *Lute* is likely to be simply the way the English heard the word *al'ud*, which is shortened to *oud* or *ud*. Take the *a* away and the English word is practically formed. The quill plectrum remained during medieval times when the instrument was used only in ensemble or accompaniment playing. Then the neck gradually evolved with the addition of frets—strips of gut tied to the neck to create semitones. This was a big step away from its Arabian cousin, as frets took away the fluid and microtonal sound characteristic of Eastern music.

During the Renaissance, lute music in the hands of composers like John Dowland became far too sophisticated to play with a quill. Chords and fast runs could only be achieved using the fingers and thumb. Books of instruction, explaining playing technique emerged during this time.

Another evolutionary change occurred in the tuning. The oud and lute were basically tuned in fourths. During the fifteenth century one of the fourths mutated into a third. The Renaissance lute then had a single first string and five other paired strings (called *courses*). These strings were made from spun sheep gut. The tuning was GG CC FF AA DD G, the third being found in the interval between F and A.

As time went on, more strings were added in order to achieve lower bass notes. To do this, the instrument had to get bigger and stronger, with a longer and longer neck. The later *theorbo* and *chitarrone* were so big and cumbersome, as to be comical. Again, the biological analogy is appropriate here. This is comparable to the flourishing of the enormous mammals found during the Cenozoic epoch. They became too big for their own good and died out. The same is true for these lutes.

Where biology and culture differ of course, is that extinct cultural artifacts can be brought back to life. Guitarist Julian Bream and others have done much to revive the music and instrument from another time that could so easily have been forgotten. Most of the music for lute that survives is written in a complex system of tablature, which can now be written out in modern notation and modern tab.

# Arranging For The Ukulele

All the pieces in this collection have been available to classical guitarists for a long time. Most of them were originally written for the lute, or else were songs or dances that were arranged for the lute. Transposing them from guitar to ukulele was fairly easy once my initial trial and error gave way to a system. I took the melodies from the guitar scores and played them on the ukulele as if I was playing a guitar. The open first string on the guitar is an E but an A on the ukulele—a difference of four notes. All harmony notes on the guitar then were four notes out with the ukulele and had to be raised a fourth to keep the intervals the same. Once this was done, the new key had to be a fourth higher.

I have kept the notation as simple as possible, adjusting some of the complex voices and rhythms to make it easy to read. Many ukulele players will read only the tab, but notation can be useful to confirm the rhythms and I hope my recording will do the same. It also might be interesting to listen to these pieces performed on the lute.

The ukulele seems like a small but increasingly successful animal that has come out of its limited environment to adapt to new musical territory, out-living the dinosaurs and the cumbersome, overgrown creatures to sing new songs in its own sweet way. It can play music from yesterday just as beautifully as it is bound to play new music from modern-day composers who recognize the huge potential of such a tiny instrument.

# From Lute To Uke

Thanks to the amazing contributions of John King, Colin Tribe, Lyle Ritz, Jake Shimabukuro, the Ukulele Orchestra of Great Britain and many others, the ukulele has truly come to life in many genres of music. Like the guitar, it is a solo instrument with many expressive qualities. The crisp, rich sound of the ukulele beautifully imitates several early instruments, including the harp, the lute, the hurdy-gurdy and the vihuela and has the advantage of being far easier (and less expensive!) to play than any of them.

Listening to Béla Fleck play Bach on the banjo is all that one needs to dispel the view that music should only be performed on the instrument for which it was written. In his hands, the banjo immediately transforms into a Baroque lute. I hope these pieces will have a similar effect on your uke.

# About The Arrangements

**Bear Dance:** A traditional European tune, possibly of Flemish origin that uses just six notes. This piece sounds good on a variety of instruments, including the fiddle, concertina and mandolin. *YouTube* has some fine examples.

**Schiarazula Marazula:** A pagan-sounding piece composed by Renaissance Italian composer, Giorgio Mainerio. His interest in the occult led to an investigation by The Inquisition, but the charges were dropped through lack of evidence.

**Orlando Sleepeth:** This is the first and easiest of the eight John Dowland lute compositions in this collection. An intriguing title that makes you want to know more. It is likely that there is some connection to the epic poem "Orlando Furioso" by Ludovico Ariosto where the hero is driven mad by the betrayal of a loved one. In 1592, Robert Greene published *The History of Orlando Furioso*. In this version, Orlando is given a potion to make him sleep and to restore his sanity. Dowland's title for this piece seems to reflect this part of the poem.

**Pavana:** Luis de Milán was a Spanish composer who wrote this piece for the "Spanish lute" or vihuela. This six stringed instrument developed in part due to the antipathy the Spanish felt towards the lute that, understandably, they associated with the invading Moors and their ouds! In distancing themselves from the oud, the Spanish allowed the vihuela to gradually evolve into the "Spanish" or classical guitar and, of course, the brighter sounding flamenco guitar that retains some oud-like qualities.

**Bransle de Champagne:** This is an example of the composer's many dances. A stirring tune, not without its difficulties on the ukulele. Barring the G chord frees up finger four to stretch to the fifth fret when needed. The D major chord at the beginning of measure 15 is best played with the first finger holding down strings 4 and 3, and the second finger holding down the second string. This leaves the third and fourth fingers free to play other notes.

**My Lord Willoughby's Welcome Home:** Dowland wrote this piece based upon an Elizabethan ballad about Francis Willoughby, a commander during the English civil war. There are many other versions of the same piece.

**Les Bouffons:** This is a four-person sword dance and translates to "The Clowns" in English. If you think "Thoinot" is an odd name, you would be right. This French composer and choreographer used an anagram of his real name—Jehan Tabourot when writing music. He was very interested in dance and wrote extensively on dance steps and styles. If you strum this tune throughout with your index finger, the sound takes on the quality of a hurdy-gurdy.

**Mr. Dowland's Midnight:** This is the first of two melancholy pieces that so define Dowland's compositions. Dowland's songs are saturated with sadness, loss and despair. The expression of such emotions was perhaps as much a part of the culture of his time as his personality. It's very easy to play on the ukulele and consequently easy to express that "midnight" feeling.

**Der Haupff Auff:** A German lutenist and composer wrote this lively dance. This piece and the next are very easy to play and adapt for the ukulele. The bouncy, dotted rhythm throughout this piece makes it particularly enjoyable to play.

**Welscher Tanz:** A very similar piece to the previous one, but this time the eighth notes are not dotted, giving a feeling of "busyness" and ongoing movement. The title translates into "The Dance of the Washer Woman," so perhaps this impression was intended. Again, no more than four simple chords with a tune wrapped around them.

**Allemande:** *Allemande*, meaning *German* in French, is a dance that accentuates the second beat of the bar. This one is simple and elegant with that typical ending on a major chord instead of a minor. As time went on, many of these dances became just too complex to dance to and became compositions in their own right, marking the evolution towards the Baroque era, exemplified by Bach. It's quite satisfying to strum many of these chords instead of plucking them.

**Round Battle Galliard:** Another piece by Dowland. Here the dotted rhythms and repeated notes evoke marching soldiers and military drum beats. On the ukulele, the music sounds more cheerful than war-like!

**Kemp's Jig:** In 1598, Will Kemp was bet £100 that he couldn't dance for 100 miles. He took on the challenge and danced from London to Norwich in nine days, keeping a diary as he went. "Kemp's Jig" was written to celebrate this remarkable achievement.

**Pastime With Good Company:** Written more than five hundred years ago, this wonderful song cannot be matched. Unlike "Greensleeves," which is commonly believed to be, but probably wasn't written by Henry the VIII, this song certainly was. Henry was a great sportsman and musician and was fond of "making merry" when he wasn't sending his wives to the chopping block. This piece sounds good with a drum accompaniment, or get a friend to clap or tap the back of his or her ukulele!

**Tarleton's Resurrection:** Richard Tarleton was a court jester for Elizabeth I. He was also an actor and playwright and was involved in Shakespeare's plays. His death was greatly mourned and Dowland wrote this piece in honor of him to keep his memory alive. He was obviously successful in this, as this tune is still being played five hundred years later! Where possible, I fleshed out some of the harmony with chords in this arrangement.

**Ballett:** One of over three hundred dances from *Terpsichore*—a volume of secular music produced by Praetorius, a German composer and organist who wrote a great deal of sacred music. His *Terpsichore* ("love of dance") is his only surviving secular collection. This piece is very popular with guitarists. It has a lovely, elegant melody that works perfectly on the ukulele and was written without specific instruments in mind. I have simplified this piece for the ukulele without losing its essential charm.

**La Volta:** A really simple dance tune, based on three chords. Detailed instructions on how to perform this dance were provided by Thoinot Arbeau (see "Les Buffons.") The dance involves the man briefly lifting the lady up into the air. An easy, but effective piece to play on the ukulele.

**Canción del Emperador:** This piece was arranged for lute by Luys de Narváez, a sixteenth century Spanish lutenist. The Emperor to which the title refers is Charles V and this piece is said to be his favorite song. This is one of the two longer pieces that I have arranged. It is enjoyable to play on the guitar and I was determined to make it work on the ukulele. In several places, I ran out of notes and had to move the tune up an octave. I played it quite slowly as this is a deep and profound piece of music that needs to be savored and absorbed.

**Almayne:** This piece is the first of the more challenging pieces in this collection. Nonetheless it's a joyful, fun dance by the English composer Francis Cutting. There are several places where it is vital to hold down a barré with the first finger. I have indicated these places with the traditional Roman numerals (CII, CV, etc.) to show what fret needs to be held down.

**Melancholy Galliard:** One of Dowland's deeply forlorn pieces. Why sadness in music is also beautiful is a question I have often asked, but never had a satisfactory answer. Dowland seems to have asked the same question through one of his songs "I Saw My Lady Weep" in which he expresses a conflict of emotion—it hurts to see her so sad, and yet her tears are something beautiful to behold. You wouldn't want to play this piece at a friendly get-together, but in a quiet, reflective moment, you can really pour your feelings into this tune.

**A Toy:** In a musical context, "A Toy" is a "plaything"—a not very serious tune! On the guitar, this is a very easy tune to play but it has come out harder on the ukulele. I have arranged it so that much of the fingerboard is used with some higher pitched notes, which, I think, makes it sound more playful.

**The Shoemaker's Wife:** Shoemakers had a strong positive image during Elizabethan times. Dowland probably had this image in mind when he composed the piece. The Elizabethan play *The Shoemaker's Holiday* by Thomas Dekker may also have had an influence. The result is a gentle tune, rather like a musical portrait.

**Bransle de la Royne:** "The Queen's Dance" is another piece from Praetorius' *Terpsichore*. There are some fairly difficult bars that require a finger 1 barré but, as with so many of these pieces, the rhythm is simple and elegant.

**Allemande (My Lady Hunssdon's Puffe):** In stark contrast to the "Melancholy Galliard," this piece is the polar opposite in mood. It seems like a huge outpouring of happiness and humor. The "puffe" probably refers to the exertion and heavy breathing that is needed to dance this Almain. Some of the repeated chords seem to suggest a feeling of getting out of breath. There are several compositions by Dowland with similar joyful moods that make you wonder if he was "bi-polar."

# Some Notes On The Symbols Used In The Music

Most classical guitarists tend to ignore much of the left-hand fingering suggestions given in their music. In fact, at a master class I attended years ago, the advice was to scrub out the fingerings as soon as you buy a new piece of music and put in your own! With this in mind, I have kept the "clutter" in this collection to the bare minimum. In places however, I have put in some fingerings 1–4 where I think it might be helpful.

I have also indicated where it is necessary to barré a chord. The traditional way to indicate this is by Roman numerals. CIV, for example means, hold down fret 4 with a first finger barré. If you find a way that feels better for you, go for it! Likewise, if you find that one or two notes are too difficult to play, omit them or change them. Professional guitarists do this all the time.

In "Allemande (My Lady Hunssdon's Puffe)," you will see the following symbol  several times in the notation. This indicates that the main note is decorated by playing the main note, the note above it and back again to the main note in one rapid movement. Any music dictionary will provide more details on ornamentation.

With regards to the right hand, it's interesting to be aware that the lute was not played with fingernails, (unless you are Julian Bream). However, a much better tone can be achieved on the ukulele with smoothly polished nails that project beyond the fingertips, as well as making the strings easier to pluck. If Julian Bream feels that life is too short to be worrying about authentic purity, I think we can safely do the same.

## References:

*Instruments of the Middle Ages and Renaissance* by David Munrow, Oxford University Press

*An Introduction to Lute Playing* by Diana Poulton, Schott & Co., Ltd

*Discover Early Music* by Lucien Jenkins, Naxos Books

*Grove's Dictionary of Music and Musicians,* ed: H. C. Colles, Macmillan & Co.

# Bear Dance

Anonymous
(c.1500 - 1600)

TRACK 1

Ukulele

* The four lower lines depict the strings of the ukulele, the bottom line representing
   the fourth or "G" string, etc. The numerals on these lines indicate the fret at which
   the string is to be pressed down. 0 indicates an open string (no fingers).

4

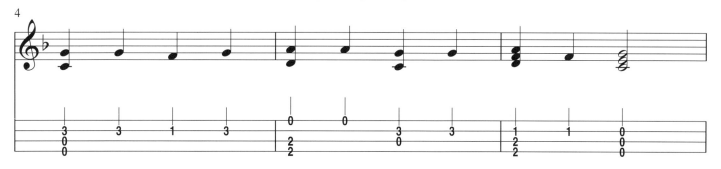

7

10

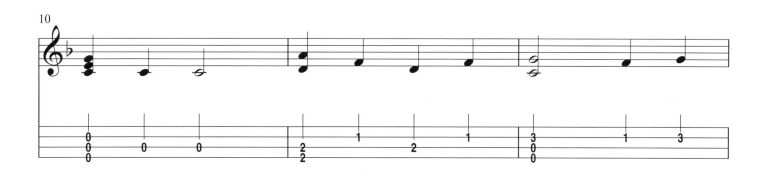

13

# Schiarazula Marazula

TRACK 2

Giorgio Mainerio
(1535-1582)

Ukulele

# Orlando Sleepeth

John Dowland
(1562-1626)

TRACK 3

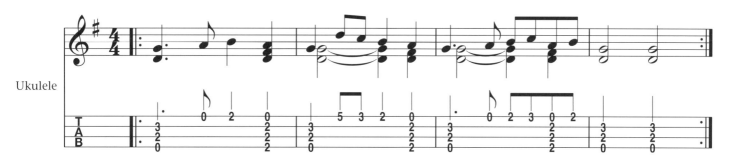

Ukulele

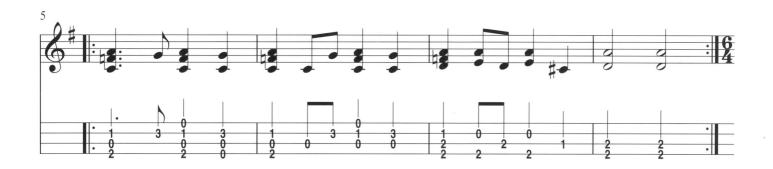

# Pavana

Luis de Milán
(c.1500-1561)

TRACK 4

Ukulele

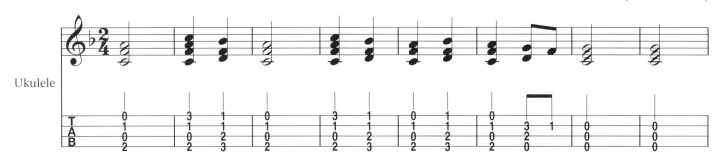

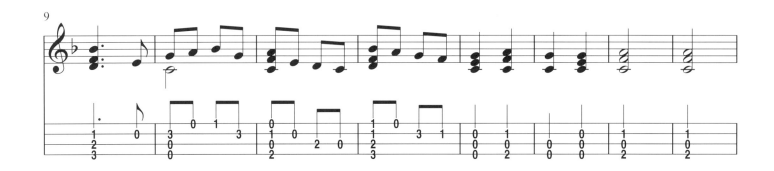

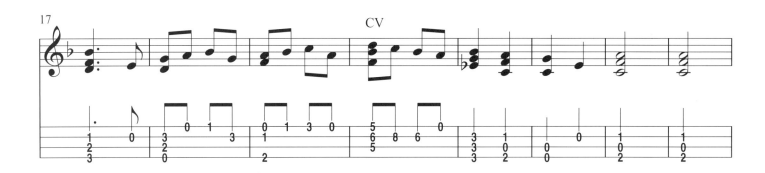

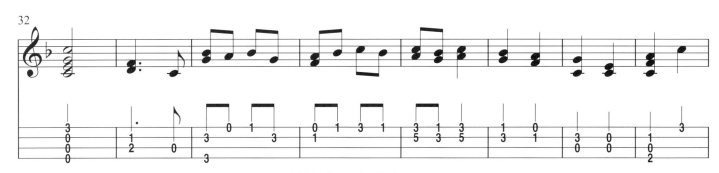

# Bransle de Champagne

Claude Gervaise
(c.1520-1580)

TRACK 5

Ukulele

# My Lord Willoughby's Welcome Home

TRACK 6

John Dowland
(1562-1626)

Ukulele

# Les Bouffons

Thoinot Arbeau
(1520-1595)

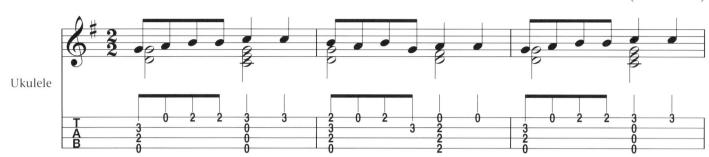

Ukulele

*Fine*

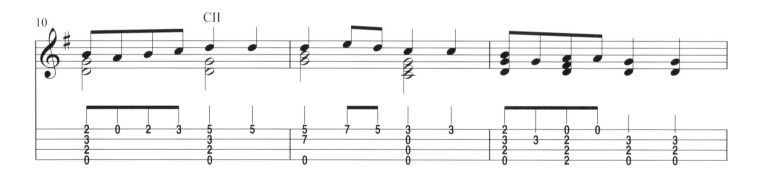

CII

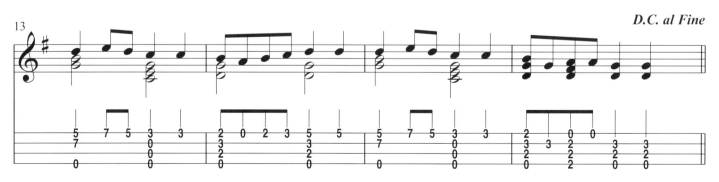

*D.C. al Fine*

# Mr. Dowland's Midnight

John Dowland
(1562-1626)

TRACK 8

Ukulele

# Der Haupff Auff

TRACK 9

Hans Neusiedler
(1508-1536)

# Welscher Tanz

Hans Neusiedler
(1508-1536)

Ukulele

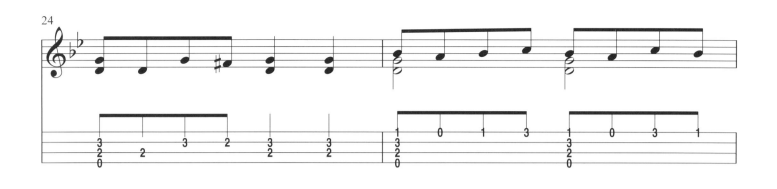

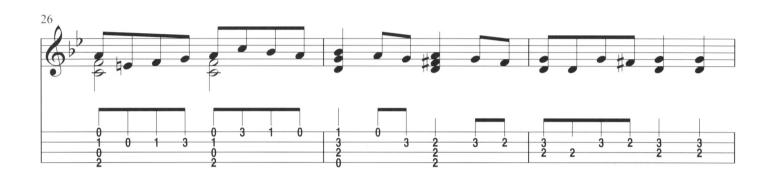

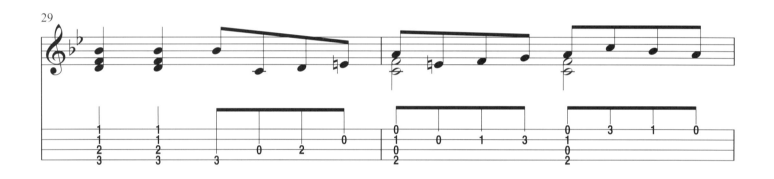

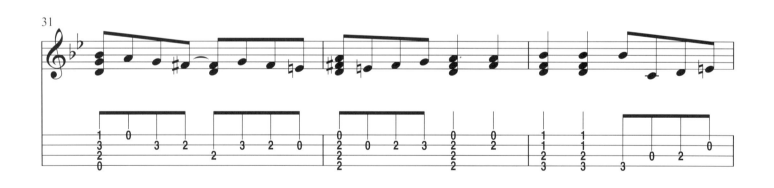

# Allemande

TRACK 11

Anonymous
(c.1500-1600)

Ukulele

# Round Battle Galliard

John Dowland
(1562-1626)

Ukulele

# Kemp's Jig

Anonymous
(c.1500-1600)

TRACK 13

Ukulele

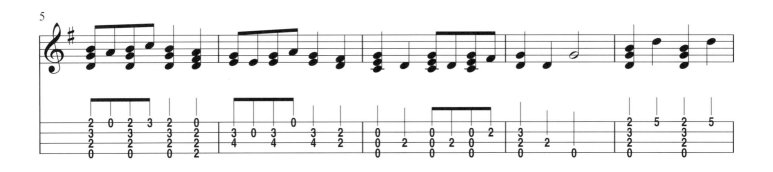

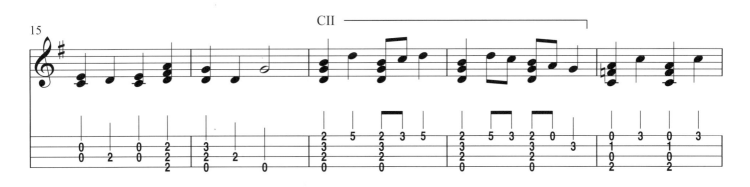

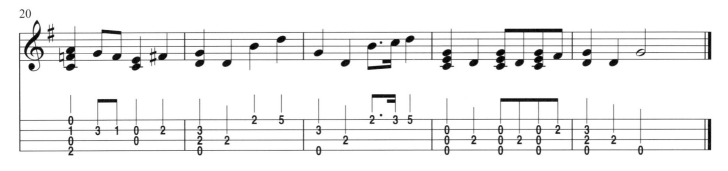

# Pastime With Good Company

Henry VIII
(1491-1547)

Ukulele

# Tarleton's Resurrection

TRACK 15

John Dowland
(1562-1626)

Ukulele

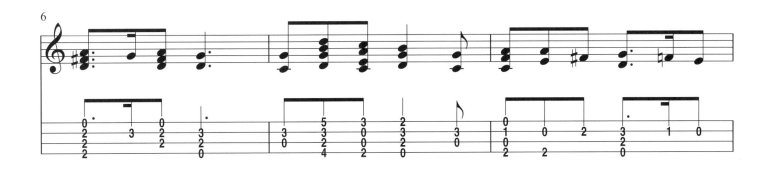

# Ballett

Michael Praetorius
(1572-1621)

Ukulele

# La Volta

# Canción del Emperador

TRACK 18

Josquin des Prés
(c.1450-1521)

Ukulele

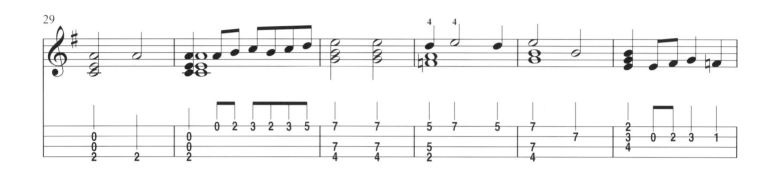

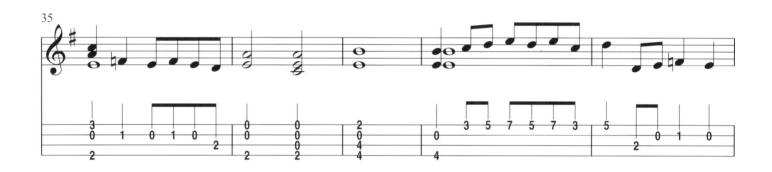

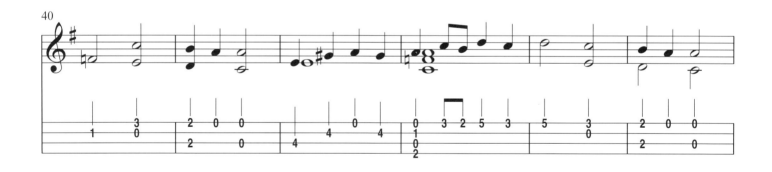

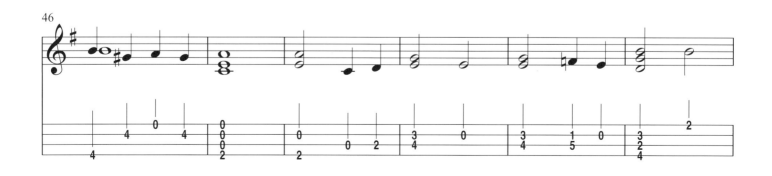

# Almayne

Francis Cutting
(1550-1595)

TRACK 19

Ukulele

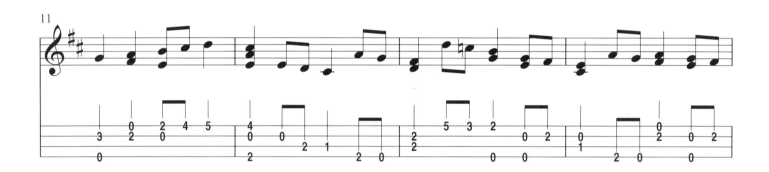

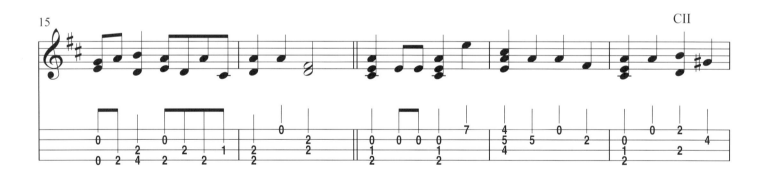

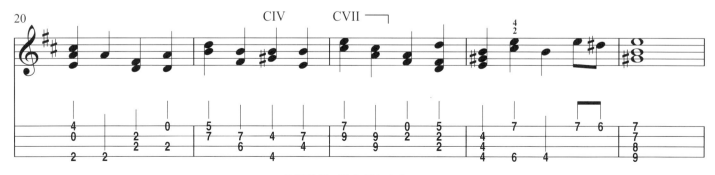

# Melancholy Galliard

TRACK 20

John Dowland
(1562-1626)

# A Toy

Anonymous
(c.1500-1600)

TRACK 21

Ukulele

# The Shoemaker's Wife

John Dowland
(1562-1626)

TRACK 22

Ukulele

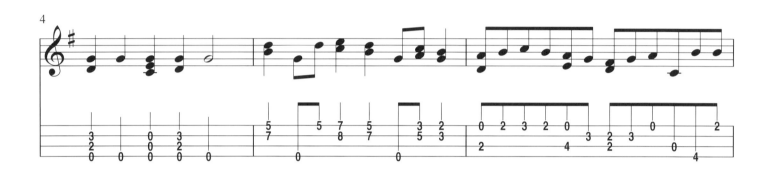

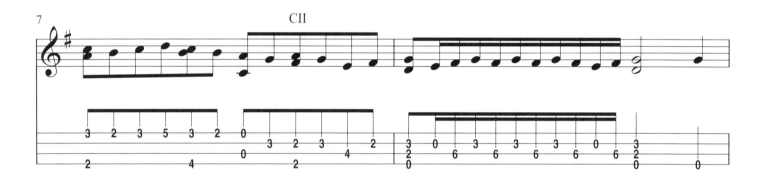

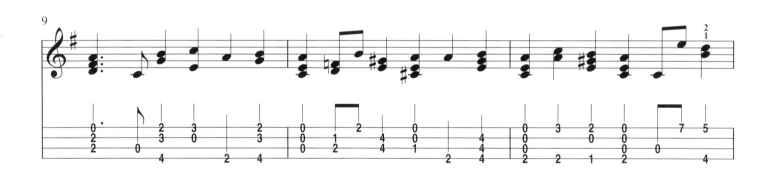

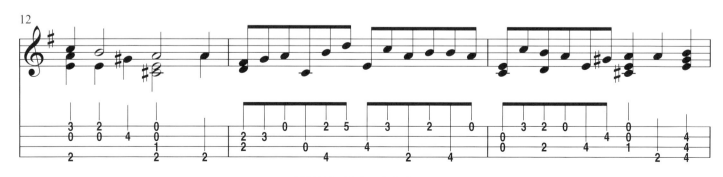

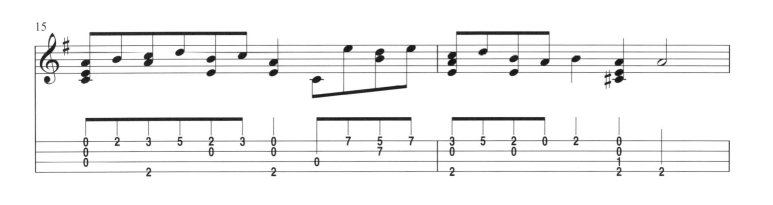

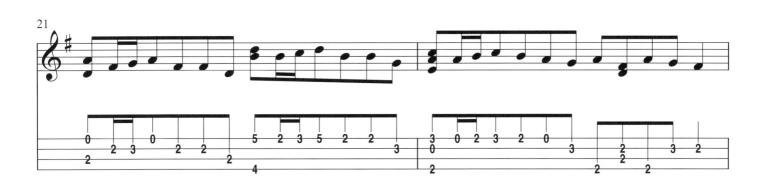

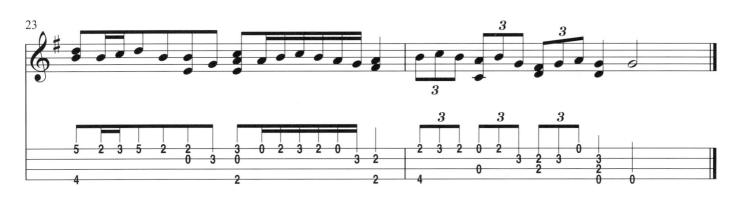

# Bransle de la Royne

Michael Praetorius
(1572-1621)

TRACK 23

Ukulele

# Allemande
## (My Lady Hunssdon's Puffe)

John Dowland
(1562-1626)

Ukulele